Escaping the Haunting Past

Escaping the Haunting Past

A HANDBOOK FOR DELIVERANCE

Chris Palmer

LIGHT OF TODAY
PUBLISHING

Copyright © 2016 Chris Palmer
All rights reserved.

ISBN: 1537110888
ISBN 13: 9781537110882
Library of Congress Control Number: 2016914075
CreateSpace Independent Publishing Platform
North Charleston, South Carolina

To those desperate for a new life…

His name is Jesus.

Whoever is a believer in Christ is a new creation. The old way of living has disappeared. A new way of living has come into existence. –2 Corinthians 5:17

Contents

Introduction ix
What is Deliverance? xi
Should I Go Through Deliverance? xv
Understanding Demons and Their Activity xix
How To Be Sure Deliverance Will Work xxiii

Part 1 Is Jesus the Lord and Savior of Your Life? 1
Part 2 Belief System 5
Part 3 Unforgiveness 10
Part 4 Generational Curses 16
Part 5 Sins of the Flesh 22
Part 6 Mental and Emotional Issues 30
Part 7 Pride and Rebellion 35
Part 8 Receive the Baptism in the Holy Spirit 41

        Maintaining Your Deliverance 45
        Final Charge 47
        Notes 49

Introduction

Dear Friend—

At Light of Today, it is our desire for you to become everything that God's Word says that you can be in Christ Jesus. We want you to be totally whole: in body, mind, soul, and spirit. No matter what you have done and despite what your past looks like, this is possible through faith in God's Word and the transforming power of the Holy Spirit.

One of the greatest steps you can take toward overcoming the effects of your former life is to experience deliverance. Deliverance is not an excessive practice unfounded in the Word of God. Rather, it is completely Scriptural. This handbook will explain to you everything you need to know about it from the Bible and will guide you through the process of deliverance in your own life.

I have seen tremendous results in the lives of those who have gone through deliverance; they drop addictions and bad habits more easily, they have more strength over their flesh and emotions, their walk with the Lord becomes closer, they are far less likely to backslide into their old ways, and they bear more fruit for God's Kingdom.

It is important to take this seriously; do it by faith from your heart, exercise your will, and believe that God will heal you from the past. If you just go through the motions, saying everything mechanically, it will not produce any change in your life. That's because this manual is not a book of secret formulas — no such thing exists. Rather, it's a guide that helps you turn your faith in the right direction.

May God bless you richly for reaching out to him to make you whole. According to your faith, be it unto you.

Maranatha

Chris Palmer

What is Deliverance?

When an individual comes to the Lord, the Bible says that they become a new person in Christ; the old life is gone, a new life has begun (2 Corinthians 5:17). This is called being born again (John 3:3). When you are born again, you also receive the indwelling of the Holy Spirit — God's Spirit comes to live inside of you. You are adopted into God's family and an everlasting inheritance awaits you in Heaven (Romans 8:16; 1 Peter 1:4). These realities are yours, even if you don't feel like they are. In fact, much of our new life in Christ is based upon discovering our identity in him.

Being born again, however, does not mean that every problem that we have ever experienced just goes away. Speaking about our bodies, for example, someone who gets saved with a broken arm will still have that broken arm after their conversion. They may continue seeing a doctor to help them treat their injury until it heals. In the same way, an individual who has emotional, mental, or spiritual problems may continue experiencing them after they are saved. *Deliverance is the process used to confront these issues and bring freedom, relief, and wholeness.*

Deliverance is accomplished in four main ways: repenting of and renouncing the issue or sin, affirming who you are in Christ, submitting to God, and renewing your mind. Without all four of these working together, it is not true deliverance.

What Is Repentance (2 Corinthians 7:9-10)?

Repentance means *a change of mind* concerning sin. It includes heartfelt sorrow toward sin that has been committed, followed by a commitment to forsake it and to follow Christ instead. Repentance implies several things:

- *An intellectual understanding that sin is wrong:* It makes sense to you that sin is stupid and a poor choice.
- *Emotional approval regarding God's Word:* Your inner man longs to walk away from sin and follow God.

- *A decision of the will:* Your will orders you away from sin and unto God.
- *Action:* You start following God's commands.

What Is Renunciation (Proverbs 28:13; 2 Corinthians 4:2)?

Renunciation or to renounce something means *to give up by way of a formal declaration*. In other words, *to bid farewell to something*. Second Corinthians 4:2 talks about renouncing *the hidden things of dishonesty*. The hidden things of dishonesty refer to the hidden areas of our lives that cause shame and disgrace. The longer these areas are left hidden, the more they grow and the more of a problem they become. This is because they are open doors that the devil uses to harass and torment. By verbally renouncing these areas, you confront them at the root and formally remove their place out of your life, along with any evil spirit associated with them.

What Is Affirming Who You Are in Christ (Ephesians 1:17-18; Philemon 1:6)?

A victorious Christian life comes from agreeing with God's Word. Just reading what God says about us doesn't necessarily mean that we agree with it. We agree with it when we confess it from our mouths, affirming that it is true in our lives. Doing this constantly establishes our identity in Christ and keeps us from establishing our identity in the world or upon Satan's lies. The more we confess and affirm God's Word, the more we become what he desires for us to be — and the less likely are we to be drawn away by any kind of deception.

What Is Submitting to God (James 4:7)?

Submitting to God simply means recognizing God's Word as the highest authority and obeying it. It also means resisting the devil and our former lives of sin. Bondage is the result of disobedience; blessing is the result of obedience. You cannot walk liberated and, at the same time, be disobedient to God. Therefore, deliverance requires a lifestyle of obedience, even when it's challenging to obey. A life submitted to God (a holy lifestyle) is the greatest defense against the enemy.

What Is Renewing the Mind (Romans 12:1-2)?

Renewing the mind means cleaning up our minds and training them to think the way that God thinks. The unrenewed mind is polluted with unbiblical worldviews, negativity, self-centeredness, and Satan's lies. By setting our minds on things from above (Colossians 3:1), our thinking changes and we begin to see ourselves *in Christ* — the way God sees us. Only when we see ourselves this way can we experience the abundant Christian life that Jesus desires for us to have. Therefore, deliverance is an ongoing, daily process of filling our minds with God's truth.

DELIVERANCE IS AN ENCOUNTER WITH TRUTH

It is commonly assumed that deliverance from demons has to be a radical and stentorian experience. While it is true that people can manifest demons in various ways during a deliverance session, this isn't always the case. Sometimes a session comes and goes and there is no physical evidence that deliverance is taking place. It all depends on the issue and level of bondage an individual is experiencing.

Because of wrong teaching, some have a tendency to believe that if there is no demonic manifestation, deliverance hasn't worked. This is not true! Bondage is broken when Satan's lies are overcome by God's truth, regardless of what a person experiences when this happens. Therefore, the focus of each session should be exposing Satan's lies and replacing them with God's truth, and not what takes place when that is going on.

Jesus said, *And you will know the truth, and the truth will set you free* (John 8:32). Satan was defeated and disarmed at the cross (Colossians 2:15). Now, Jesus has all power and authority (Matthew 28:18). As a result, the only way Satan can work is through deception. In fact, the Scriptures call him a deceiver (Revelation 12:9). These deceptions are what take people captive and hold them in bondage. No matter what the issue, true deliverance is taking place in a person's heart when they confront what is holding them in bondage and then submits to God.

Paul's desire for the Ephesian believers was that their understanding be filled with the truth in Christ (Ephesians 1:17-23). This is the ultimate aim of deliverance and is, therefore, the goal of each session.

As you go through deliverance, it is important to keep these things in mind so that you are conscious of what needs to be done. This will help ensure you have a fruitful result.

Should I Go Through Deliverance?

WHAT KIND OF INDIVIDUAL SHOULD be seeking to go through deliverance? The fact is that people from all walks of life go through deliverance; each situation is unique. Some have been Christians their whole lives, while others have had backgrounds in the occult and false religion. Some have serious habits and addictions, while others have quite ordinary behavioral patterns. So how can you determine if it is something for *you*? While the decision is ultimately yours to make, taking time to work through deliverance is something every single believer should do, no matter what one's involvement in past sin has looked like.

IS IT BIBLICAL?

Yes. While you will not find an example of believers sitting through a deliverance session in the New Testament, there are more than enough references in the Bible that teach us to put a high premium on repenting, renouncing, affirming our identity in Christ, submitting to God, and renewing our minds. Being the case, can't that be done in a session? Of course, it can. Consider also:

- *After the Ephesian believers were converted, they burnt their occult books.* Notice:

    Many who became believers confessed their sinful practices. A number of them who had been practicing sorcery brought their incantation books and burned them at a public bonfire. The street value of the books was several million dollars. So the message about the Lord spread widely and had a powerful effect. –Acts 19:19-20

    This is an example of renouncing the old life and leaving it behind. During deliverance, we ask counselees to do the same — destroy any objects in their possession that represent the former life.

- *After believing in the Gospel and being baptized into water, Simon the sorcerer still had issues with sin — he was attracted to esoteric things and desired to exploit them for money.* When the apostle Peter discovered this, he told Simon to repent and pray to the Lord as the means to finding deliverance from his evil thoughts, inward weaknesses, and sinful practices. Peter instructed Simon to seek God's help in the specific areas where he was struggling (Acts 8:12-23). When Christians are struggling in specific areas, deliverance helps them to hone in on them, and to seek God for his help.
- *History tells us that the ancient church verbally renounced Satan, gave allegiance to God, and affirmed the fundamental doctrines of Christianity before being water baptized.[1]* This manner of renunciation and affirmation is what we are practicing in deliverance.

DELIVERANCE IS FOR YOU IF:

- *You are having bouts with certain sins and have been unsuccessful in overcoming them.*
- *You are experiencing mental and emotional turmoil.*
- *You are suffering from your past.*
- *You have unresolved anger and frustration in your heart toward another individual.*
- *You have not been able to find your identity.*
- *You are constantly distracted while praying or reading the Bible.*
- *You are rebellious and bitter toward the Church.*
- *Despite your best effort, you just can't seem to grow any further in the Lord.*
- *Constant failure in everything you try.*
- *You are focused on your past: talking about it and thinking about it too much.*

SHOULD I GO THROUGH DELIVERANCE AGAIN?

The biggest part of deliverance is renewing your mind. No matter how much freedom you discover during a deliverance session, it will not be rightly maintained if you don't read and study the Word of God daily.

God's Word is our spiritual food (Matthew 4:4). If we fail to receive spiritual nourishment, we will become spiritually weak and fall back into our old ways. Hence, if you have issues after deliverance, it is likely that you have not been renewing your mind. If that is the case, what you need most is a daily commitment to God's Word (Acts 2:42) and not another deliverance session.

---

[1] Robert E. Webber. *Liturgical Evangelism. (Harrisburg, PA: More House Pub Co., 1992)*, 90-92.

Perhaps you make the same mistake again after deliverance. Should you come back for more deliverance? No. You should go to God and express your godly sorry (2 Corinthians 7:10), confess that what you have done is sin, renounce it, and ask God for his forgiveness and the help of the Holy Spirit (1 John 1:9). Then you should immediately begin renewing your mind and affirming who you are in Christ.

The only time someone should seek deliverance again is if they go through a season of backsliding that puts them into bondage. In this case, there may be some deeper issues going on that have led to demonic influences.

CAN I TAKE MYSELF THROUGH DELIVERANCE?

It is possible if you are a believer, yes. This is because every believer has authority in Christ and is full of the power of the Holy Spirit. Therefore, a believer can repent of and renounce their sin, submit to God, affirm who they are in Christ, and renew their mind without the help of another individual. Self-deliverance is a good option when:

- *You are a spiritual leader (pastor, minister, elder, etc.) and cannot find anyone more mature than yourself to take you through deliverance.* (It is important to note that deliverance should never be done with someone you cannot trust. If you are a leader, you should only go through deliverance with another leader, preferably someone equal or higher than you.)
- *You don't know or can't find any people or ministries that believe in deliverance.*

If you desire to go through self-deliverance, it is important to:

- *Do it in private:* This is not anyone's business but your own; it is between you and the Lord.
- *Work together with the Holy Spirit:* Trust the Holy Spirit to reveal areas where you need deliverance. Recognize that his power is present and that you aren't doing it in your own strength.
- *Be patient and don't be in a hurry:* Set aside plenty of time to do this. Sometimes it takes a while to break certain strongholds. Being in a rush will hinder the process.
- *Take authority over any attack:* It's possible the enemy might attack you to keep you from being free. You may start hearing voices speaking to your mind, experience shortness of breath, get antsy and nervous, become overwhelmed by emotion, or be overcome with some other physical symptom. Should this happen, remember that you have *authority*. Greater is he that is in you than he that is in the world (1 John 4:4).

Stop for a moment, take authority over the enemy, ask the Holy Spirit to help you regain yourself, and continue.

If you *can* find someone who qualifies to take you through deliverance, you should go with this option based upon the accountability principle found in James 5:16, *Confess your faults one to another, and pray one for another, that ye may be healed.*

When we are overwhelmed with struggle, it is often because our own strength is not enough. In cases like this, God desires for us to link our faith to another believer's faith and overcome together. Deuteronomy 32:30 teaches us that there is strength in numbers; that one can put 1,000 to flight but two can put 10,000 to flight. Jesus taught that there is power in praying in agreement (Matthew 18:18-20). No Christian can do it alone; we need each other and we draw strength from one another.

Don't Talk About Your Deliverance With Everyone

It is imperative not to talk openly about the details of your deliverance. This is because:

- *Certain issues create stigmas:* A stigma is a mark of disgrace. Not everyone you tell your past problems to will receive you the way that you might hope, or the way that they should. Instead, they may put a label on you and even gossip about you, particularly if they are immature.
- *It doesn't do you any good to announce your past issues to everyone:* James 5:16 says that believers are to confess their problems *one to another*, not one to everyone. You are no freer because you share with everyone.
- *Wait a while to prove your deliverance*: Before we give testimonies of inner healing and deliverance, it is wise to allow time to prove it out. In many instances it is hard to see the full impact of deliverance right away.

Understanding Demons and Their Activity

Having a Biblical understanding about demons and their activity is essential for every believer in Christ. This is because there exists so much misunderstanding concerning them. It isn't rare to see excessive teaching about demons in one place and no teaching about demons in another. Both are incorrect and unbiblical. God's Word doesn't indict demons as the cause behind every single problem in the world. But God's Word is extremely clear that demons do cause many of the problems and issues people experience in their everyday lives.

Here are some biblical principles about demons that will clear up your understanding about demons and help you determine if they have been problematic in your own life.

Christians *Cannot* Be Demon Possessed

Demonic possession is the complete and total control of demons over an individual — body, soul, and spirit. The individual under demonic possession is inhabited by demons and has lost his will and inhibitions (Mark 5:1-20). A Christian is one who has died to sin (Romans 6:11), received the indwelling of the Holy Spirit (1 Corinthians 3:16), and is a saint — meaning a holy one of God (1 Corinthians 1:2). Considering what a true Christian is from Scripture, it is not possible to believe that one can be demon possessed. Certainly the Holy Spirit and demonic beings cannot share the same vessel.

Christians *Can* Experience Oppression, Depression, and/or Obsession Because of Demonic Influence

Though Jesus has come and destroyed the control of sin in the lives of those who put their faith and trust in him (1 John 3:8), demons still persist in their work upon the earth. Therefore, demons *must* be resisted (James. 4:7). This is done using the armor of God (Ephesians 6:11). If a believer fails to use their armor and authority in Christ, they can become victim to demonic influence. Some of the most common symptoms of demonic influence are:

- *Oppression:* Constant mental torment; persistent psychological and emotional unrest.
- *Depression:* Heavy feelings of sadness, worthlessness, and the lack of desire to do daily activities.
- *Obsession:* The domination of an individual's thoughts by a constant desire, image, or idea.

Ways Demons Can Gain Access Into a Person's Life

Demonic influence cannot occur in the life of a believer unless the believer gives Satan place. This can be done in ignorance or out of rebellion. Either way, Satan will take full advantage of it. Here are some of the most common things that Christians suffer because of:

- *Unforgiveness*: Holding a grudge toward someone is idolatry. This gives demons an opportunity to torment us (Matthew 18:21-35).
- *Personal sin:* Satan tries to access our lives through temptation. Therefore, Christians have the responsibility to deny the passions of the flesh (Galatians 5:24).
- *Generational bondage*: While God does not hold us responsible for the sins of others, those sins can affect our outlook on life and behavior (Exodus 20:5).
- *Past hurts*: Wounds from the past can damage our identity, causing us to believe the lies of Satan rather than the truth of God's Word. These lies create a constant cycle of defeat and keep us from experiencing total victory in Christ (Psalm 147:3).
- *False doctrines, false religions, and an ungodly worldview*: Any belief system that contradicts the Word of God is antichrist and anathema. This is because these beliefs are literally inspired by demons that are vying for the hearts and minds of humanity (1 Timothy 4:1). Giving credence to them opens up a door for the further work of demons.
- *Not repenting for sin:* Carrying on in life without repentance will cause your heart to become hard. When this happens, demons can cause all kinds of devastation in your life (1 Corinthians 5:5).
- *Disobedience:* When we are obedient to God, he can protect us. However, disobedience takes us out of God's will, even to the point where he cannot protect us anymore. Disobedience destroys God's blessing and causes pain and regret (1 Samuel 15).

Common Symptoms Indicating Demonic Influence

How do you know that your issue is demonic? The Bible indicates a number of common symptoms:

- *Constant sickness*: Though not all sickness is caused by the presence of a demonic entity, many sicknesses are. Perplexing symptoms, numerous illnesses at the same time, and pain without cause are a few reasons to suspect that a sickness may be demonic in nature (Matthew 12:22).
- *Self-inflicted injury*: Harming oneself and desiring or trying to commit suicide (Mark 5:5).
- *Perverseness*: Practicing illicit sexual behaviors outside of God's Word; an uncontrollable appetite for sexual gratification (Mark 5:12).
- *Compulsions*: Irresistible urges to behave a certain way (Mark 5:5).
- *Inner anguish*: The inability to live with yourself due to severe distress or fear (Mark 5:5).
- *Unexplainable failure*: Nothing goes right in business, family, relationships, ministry, etc.
- *Substance abuse*: Dependence on prescription drugs, narcotics, alcohol, nicotine, sugar, etc. to deal with the anxieties and stresses of life.
- *Insomnia*: Failure to rest peacefully at night and wake up refreshed (Mark 5:5).
- *Violence and rage*: Acting violently and/or talking about harming and killing others (Mark 5:4).
- *Mental illness*: Multiple personalities, paranoia, loss of reality, etc.
- *Loneliness and isolation*: The preference to separate and detach from society and relationships (Mark 5:2).
- *Obsession with death*: Becoming fixed on dying and things associated with death.

Bondage and Strongholds

Those struggling with demonic problems are in *bondage*. Bondage is involuntary servitude and enslavement to the Kingdom of Darkness (Matthew 4:24). This is manifested through belief in false religion, ungodly practices, and sinful behavior. A person's ungodly thinking is at the root of their bondage. The Bible calls thinking that is contrary to God's Word a *stronghold* (2 Corinthians 10:4-5).

Stronghold means *fortification*. Thoughts contrary to God's Word fix themselves within the human mind and become fortified by emotion, reasoning, and passion. This means that a person is not going to experience freedom and deliverance from bondage through human strength and ability; it takes a weapon from God.

God's weapons are his Word and the power of the Holy Spirit. When we place our faith in these, they are activated in our life and begin tearing down every stronghold holding us in bondage.

During this deliverance, you have the opportunity to exercise your faith and cooperate with the Holy Spirit by repenting and affirming who you are in Christ. This begins the process of destroying the stronghold and changing your behavior. As you walk in obedience to God and renew your mind daily, strongholds continue to weaken until they have been completely removed.

How To Be Sure Deliverance Will Work

Successful deliverance requires the faith, will, and heartfelt participation of the person going through it. The minister or pastor in charge of the session may do everything in his or her power to help an individual get free and remain free. However, if the counselee is not serious or is simply going through the motions, there will be no deliverance. As a result, the individual will leave unchanged and most likely continue in their old ways. Below is a checklist of things that will ensure successful deliverance, and a checklist of things that keep deliverance from working. Prayerfully go through this to make sure that you are in position to receive deliverance.

Things That Will Ensure Successful Deliverance:

- *Expectation for God to change your life.*
- *Believing that Jesus has defeated Satan and conquered the works of darkness.*
- *A desire to leave behind the old ways and pursue God's ways.*
- *Having no confidence in your own strength and total confidence in God's strength.*
- *Complete truthfulness during the session.*
- *Praying sincerely from the heart.*
- *Respecting and trusting the minister over the session.*
- *Commitment to keep your mind renewed in order to maintain deliverance.*

Things That Will Prevent Deliverance From Working:

- *Failing/refusing to accept Jesus Christ as Lord and Savior.*
- *Believing that God does not desire to heal, deliver, and restore.*

- *Refusing to forgive.*
- *Seeking deliverance in the wrong area of your life.*
- *Believing that Christians cannot experience demonic influence (a doctrinal issue).*
- *Unconfessed sin.*
- *Denying that there is a real problem to deal with.*
- *Having a poor relationship with the minister performing the deliverance or having a problem with the church.*
- *Refusing to accept authority (this prevents the anointing from working).*
- *Occult powers that are still at work and have not been broken.*
- *Being forced to go through deliverance to appease someone else and not being there out of your own volition.*
- *Expecting nothing to happen; planning to leave and continue the same life.*
- *Not being completely truthful during the session.*
- *Apathy — not caring about the problems in your life; being passive concerning godly reform.*
- *Believing you can change yourself and do not need God's help.*

DON'T BE TOO INTROSPECTIVE

While it is important to be honest and sincere about your struggles during the session, it is just as important not to be overly analytical. For example, when you leave the session you may think *what if I forgot to mention something? Will I stay in bondage? Maybe I am not free.*

This kind of thinking is not from God; it is perfectionism and legalism and it leads to distress. Before we begin the session, we want you to pray and ask the Holy Spirit to lead and guide you into all the truth about yourself (past and present) and show you everything you need to deal with (John 14:26).

Trust the Holy Spirit and his wisdom. Decide now that you are not going to leave and later try to think up things you might have forgotten.

As we begin, pray the following prayer and commit this session totally and completely to the leadership and help of the Holy Spirit:

> **Dear Heavenly Father, I come to you now in the name of Jesus, with complete surrender. I trust in your love, your power, your mercy, and your grace. I believe that through you all things are possible, including healing and deliverance from my hurts and my past. Jesus came to destroy the works of the devil (1 John 3:8) so that I may have an abundant life (John 10:10). I acknowledge that Jesus can**

set me free from any bondage in my life and that he can make me a brand new person in him (Luke 4:18-19; 2 Corinthians 5:17), no matter what I have done or what has been done to me. Holy Spirit, search my heart and bring to light every thing that needs to be dealt with. I trust in your help and in your leadership, and I believe you will allow nothing to be left out. I pray all demonic interference, distraction, and influence be bound (Matthew 18:18-20). The blood of Jesus protects me as I go through deliverance; nothing shall prevent me from being free. In Jesus' name, Amen.

PART 1

Is Jesus the Lord and Savior of Your Life?

DELIVERANCE BEGINS WITH KNOWING JESUS Christ as Lord and Savior. Until this happens, we are under the power of darkness and servants of sin (John 8:34). Jesus said that anyone who has not experienced new life in him and adoption into God's family through faith in him is not a child of God. Rather, their father is the devil (John 8:44). This is a very serious statement.

This means that no matter how hard we try, without Jesus we will behave more or less like the devil because of sin and a sinful nature.

It's common to think that being born into the family of humanity makes us part of God's family. But the Bible doesn't teach this. It teaches us that being born again through faith in Christ makes us part of God's family (2 Corinthians 5:17; Romans 8:14-16). When we are born again, the old nature that was born in sin under Satan dies and we are given a new nature that is alive unto God (Galatians 2:20). The new life produces the fruits of good works, evidence that a transformation has taken place within (Galatians 5:22-23).

KNOWING JESUS AS LORD AND SAVIOR IS NOT:

- *Belonging to a local church or parish.*
- *Having a loved one who is close to God.*
- *Doing occasional good works.*
- *Praying once and a while.*
- *Believing in God.*
- *Considering yourself religious.*

KNOWING JESUS AS LORD AND SAVIOR IS:

- *Acknowledging that you have sinned because you are sinful (Romans 3:23).*
- *Recognizing that you cannot save yourself and need a savior from those sins.*
- *Repentance (2 Corinthians 7:9-10).*
- *Faith — deciding and trusting on Jesus to save us from our sins (Romans 10:13).*
- *Having a personal relationship with Christ, furthered through prayer, obedience, and living by faith (2 Corinthians 5:7).*

KNOWING JESUS AS LORD AND SAVIOR IS ACCOMPLISHED BY:

- *Believing in your heart that Jesus died to pay the price for your sins and rose again so that you could share eternal life with him (Romans 10:9-10).*
- *Confessing with your mouth what Jesus has accomplished and declaring that you will leave your life of sin to follow him (Romans 10:9-10; Matthew 4:19-20).*
- *Receiving by simple faith in God's grace (Ephesians 2:8).*

When you receive Jesus as Savior, you are accepting his sacrifice as payment for your sin. And when you place him as the Lord of your life you are giving him control as your ultimate authority, whom you will follow no matter what it might cost (Matthew 19:21). This brings *salvation*. Salvation is deliverance from the consequences of sin, including God's wrath.

SALVATION INCLUDES:

- *Regeneration:* The act whereby God imparts spiritual life to us. God makes us alive in Christ and gives us a new nature (Ezekiel 36:26-27; Ephesians 2:5).
- *Indwelling of the Holy Spirit:* The act whereby the Holy Spirit comes to take permanent residence inside of us (John 14:17; 1 Corinthians 6:19-20).
- *Justification*: The legal act whereby God thinks of our sins as forgiven. He declares us righteous (to have right standing with him) because he regards us as having the perfect righteousness of Christ (Romans 4:6).
- *Adoption:* The act whereby God makes us members of his family and gives to us an eternal inheritance (John 1:12; 1 John 3:1-2).
- *Glorification*: The act of receiving glorified bodies when Christ returns. Our bodies will be entirely set free from the effects of the fall and brought into the state of perfection (1 Corinthians 15:22-23).

A person who has received salvation has received authority over the works of the devil, including sin and the torment associated with sin (Ephesians 1:3, 19-23). Living in this authority comes no other way except for making Jesus the Lord and Savior of your life. Deliverance begins with this step and can't go any further until this step has been taken.

If you have never made Jesus Christ Lord and Savior of your life, do that now by profoundly praying the following prayer. (If you have been born again in the past and you haven't broken your fellowship with the Lord, you can just continue forward.)

> **Dear Heavenly Father, I come before you humbly in Jesus' name. I recognize that I am a sinner and that I am in need of your mercy and your grace. I believe that your son, Jesus Christ, came to save me from my sins because he loved me so much. I believe he died on the cross and rose again from the dead. I trust that this is sufficient to save me from sin and to give me a new life. Jesus has also called me to follow him. Today, I am leaving the old life behind and am going to follow him. Holy Spirit, come and live inside of me. You are welcome in my life. Thank you for making me new in you. I renounce the former life of sin and my ties to Satan and his kingdom. I am born again and am free from sin. I have now have authority over the works of the enemy and I will walk in it. Never again will I be taken advantage of by sin, sickness, Satan, or demons. In Jesus' name, Amen.**

If you have made Jesus the Lord and Savior of your life in the past but you have been living disobediently, this means that you are out of fellowship with the Lord. Living this way opens up your life to demonic influence and harassment; it is certain to cause misery.

Taking steps out of this misery is first done by renewing your fellowship with the Lord. It is making a fresh commitment to live obediently and to follow him. To do this, you must come to your Heavenly Father as his child, express your sorrow, ask for his forgiveness, commit to do right, and ask him for his help (1 John 1:9). Do this by praying the following prayer.

> **Dear Heavenly Father, I come to you in the name of Jesus. Although I am your child, I have made poor choices and those choices have caused me to break my fellowship with you. This has led to much difficulty, sorrow, and remorse in my life. But you have told me that if I confess my sin to you that you are faithful; you will forgive me and wash away my unrighteousness.**
>
> **I confess that I have rebelled, lived in sin apart from you, and I am truly sorry. I ask you to forgive me. I thank you for washing me clean.**

Now, I declare that you have done as your Word has said and you have forgiven me. I now stand before you cleansed. I commit to obeying you from this point forward. I ask for the help of your Holy Spirit to live for you every day. I declare that every demonic influence in my life must loose its hold, now. In Jesus' name, Amen.

Now that you have prayed and have committed yourself to the Lord, you can expect his total and complete help. God's Word says:

No, despite all these things, overwhelming victory is ours through Christ, who loved us. And I am convinced that nothing can ever separate us from God's love. Neither death nor life, neither angels nor demons, neither our fears for today nor our worries about tomorrow—not even the powers of hell can separate us from God's love. No power in the sky above or in the earth below—indeed, nothing in all creation will ever be able to separate us from the love of God that is revealed in Christ Jesus our Lord. –Romans 8:37-39

Going forward, you can expect total and complete victory over everything you deal with because the all-powerful God is on your side and he loves you and is helping you to overcome, right now!

PART 2
Belief System

SATAN SEEKS TO CONTROL OUR belief system because our belief system controls us. As you can imagine, God wants our belief system to be built upon his Word alone so that our life and practices might be under the control of the Holy Spirit. Failure to bring our minds and thinking into conformity with God's Word can turn into our participation in false religion, cults, ungodly worldviews, witchcraft, and/or the occult. These bring bondage into our lives and keep the knowledge of the truth of Christ from shining in our hearts (2 Corinthians 4:4). They are defined as follows:

- *False Religions:* Any professing of faith, system of belief, and spiritual practice that denies the Supreme Lordship of Jesus Christ as only Son of God, Savior and Lord. Also, adding to or omitting the historically and traditionally accepted and conventional doctrines of the Christian Faith[2] (1 John 2:20-23).
- *Cults:* Cults are usually smaller groups of people who maintain unconventional and strange beliefs and practices, usually religious. Their devotion is often directed toward a particular individual or fixed on a particular idea. Quite often they are harmful and sinister.
- *Ungodly Worldviews:* Any philosophy of life and concept of the world that does not adhere to God's Word, the Bible (2 Corinthians 10:4-5).
- *Witchcraft:* The practice of magic, divination, sorcery, and dark knowledge (Leviticus 19:31; Revelation 21:8), and falls under the *occult*.
- *The Occult: Occult* means hidden. It refers to a concealed set of esoteric secrets, including those darker than those practiced in witchcraft, like Satanism and its rites. Historically, these practices were kept hidden from the public eye out of fear of punishment or execution.

Those who practice and dabble in witchcraft and the occult will not see the blessing of God upon their lives in any way. In Leviticus 20:6, God says, concerning witchcraft and the occult:

---
[2] See *the Nicene Creed*.

I will also turn against those who commit spiritual prostitution by putting their trust in mediums or in those who consult the spirits of the dead. I will cut them off from the community.

Revelation 21:8 states that participation in witchcraft and the occult leads to spiritual and eternal death in the Lake of Fire: *But cowards, unbelievers, the corrupt, murderers, the immoral, those who practice witchcraft, idol worshipers, and all liars—their fate is in the fiery lake of burning sulfur. This is the second death.*

The same is true concerning false religions, cults, and ungodly worldviews. Galatians 1:8 says, *Let God's curse fall on anyone, including us or even an angel from heaven, who preaches a different kind of Good News than the one we preached to you.*

This being the case, any involvement in these needs to be renounced. Below there is a box that lists many of the common involvements people have in these. Check any of those that you have participated in, even if it was in:

- *Fun*: Out of novelty, thinking there isn't any harm in it.
- *Ignorance*: Without a proper understanding, perhaps even innocently, not knowing any better.
- *By Association*: Being present and observing, though not the primary participant.

Satan will use any means possible to access your life and destroy it. This is why we are commanded to be vigilant (1 Peter 5:8) and to avoid even the appearance of evil (1 Thessalonians 5:22).

> ### False Religions, Cults, and Ungodly Worldviews
>
> ☐ Agnosticism ☐ Atheism ☐ Baha'i ☐ Buddhism ☐ Confucianism ☐ Earth Religion
> ☐ Eckankar ☐ Free Masonry ☐ Hinduism ☐ Humanism ☐ Illuminati ☐ Islam ☐ Jainism
> ☐ Jehovah's Witness ☐ KKK ☐ Mafia ☐ Mormonism ☐ Nation of Islam ☐ New Age
> ☐ Radical Feminism ☐ Shinto ☐ Satanism ☐ Sikhism ☐ Wiccan ☐ Witchcraft ☐ Scientology
> ☐ Sikhism ☐ UFO Cults ☐ Unification Church ☐ Zoroastrianism
> ☐ Other_____
>
> ### Occult and Witchcraft Practices
>
> ☐ Astrology ☐ Astral projection ☐ Drinking Human Blood or Eating Human Flesh ☐ Fortune Telling ☐ Horoscopes ☐ Heavy Metal Music ☐ Hypnosis ☐ Magical Charms ☐ Kabbalah ☐ Levitating ☐ Mantras ☐ Mind-Altering Drugs ☐ Ouija Board ☐ Transcendental Meditation ☐ Psychic Readings ☐ Sex With a Spirit (Incubi/Succubae) ☐ Slasher/Horror Movies ☐ Spirit Guides ☐ Trances ☐ Demonic Video Games or Games (Warcraft, Pokémon, Diablo, etc.)
> ☐ Voodoo ☐ Other_____

After checking each box that pertains to you, pray the following prayer of repentance and renounce each belief and practice, specifically and individually:

Dear Heavenly Father, I come before you and humble myself in repentance. I confess that I have participated in [*false belief or false practice*]. I renounce it as false and I command every demonic spirit associated with it to go from my life. May every curse that is a result of my participation be lifted from my life and from my family's life. Thank you for your forgiveness and thank you for setting me free. Holy Spirit fill me. In Jesus' name, Amen.

After dealing with each practice, it is essential to renounce and break any *pact* or *vow* that you have made in the name of these religions or for any other purpose, contrary to following God's holy purpose for your life.

- *Pact:* A formal agreement that binds two parties together for a common purpose.
- *Vow:* A solemn promise to do a specified thing.

These are common in Satanism and other vile religions. These pacts and vows include such things as ceremonies, baptisms, blood agreements, declarations, signing treaties, taking oaths, even if they were done upon you while you were in your mother's womb. They are certain to bring demonic spirits into the lives of participants. If you have done such or have had them done to you, list each of them below:

1. _____

2. _____

3. _____

4. _____

Pray the following prayer of repentance and renounce each pact and vow specifically and individually:

In the name of Jesus, with Almighty God as my witness, I renounce and break [*pact, vow, agreement, ceremony, etc.*]. From this point forward, it is cancelled and I no longer have any more to do with it. Father, forgive me for being involved with it.

Now, I declare that I have been purchased with the blood of Jesus (1 Corinthians 6:20) and that I belong to Christ. I command every demonic spirit associated with these to go from my life. Holy Spirit, fill me to overflowing. In Jesus' name, Amen.

Now that you have renounced your former alliances with Satan, it is important to confess what you believe. There is no greater confession in the history of the Church than the Nicene Creed. The first council of Nicaea adopted this in 325 AD to establish a standard doctrinal statement to combat a great heresy known as Arianism. It was later revised in 381 AD at the first council of Constantinople. It is the only statement of faith accepted by all denominations of the Christian faith around the world: Anglican, Catholic, Coptic, Orthodox, and Protestant.

With all sincerity and faith, profess this Creed below; declare your new life that is hidden in Christ and boldly announce the hope that you have in the Kingdom of God as a holy saint in the Body of Christ.

The Nicene Creed

We believe in one God,
the Father, the Almighty,
of all that is, seen and unseen.

We believe in one Lord, Jesus Christ,
the only Son of God,
eternally begotten of the Father,
God from God, Light from Light,
true God from true God,
begotten, not made,
of one Being with the Father.
Through him all things were made.
For us and for our salvation
he came down from heaven:
by the power of the Holy Spirit
he became incarnate from the Virgin Mary,
and was made man.
For our sake he was crucified under Pontius Pilate;
he suffered death and was buried.
On the third day he rose again
in accordance with the Scriptures;
he ascended into heaven
and is seated at the right hand of the Father.
He will come again in glory to judge the living and the dead,
and his kingdom will have no end.
We believe in the Holy Spirit, the Lord, the giver of life,
who proceeds from the Father and the Son.
With the Father and the Son he is worshipped and glorified.
He has spoken through the Prophets.
We believe in one holy catholic and apostolic Church.
We acknowledge one baptism for the forgiveness of sins.
We look for the resurrection of the dead,
and the life of the world to come. Amen.

PART 3

Unforgiveness

GOD'S WORD IS CLEAR CONCERNING the importance of forgiving those who have wronged and offended us. Offense is the poisonous attitude a person takes after being slighted or injured by someone or something so that they sin in word, thought, or action. The Scriptures teach that offense is a trap and enslaves those who fall into it (Romans 9:33).

Jesus said that in this life we are sure to be offended by other people. In fact, he said it was impossible for us to live without this happening: *Then said he unto the disciples, It is impossible but that offences will come* (Luke 17:1). Therefore, we must be adamant about living our lives for Christ in a spirit of forgiveness. Forgiveness means to cancel an offender's debt out of mercy. If we don't forgive others, we will fall into the trap of offense and be enslaved by its consequences. Some of these include:

- *Torment from demons*: Demon spirits manipulate and worsen the effects of offense and, in many instances, make the pain unbearable (Matthew 18:34).
- *Hindrance to our faith*: The effectiveness of our faith is hinged upon our willingness to forgive. Faith is absolute trust in God, and forgiveness is entrusting God to deal with the offender instead of taking it upon ourselves to do so (Mark 11:22-25).
- *Satan takes advantage of our relationships*: Forgiveness puts an end to the offense and misunderstandings in our relationships, healing them. Unforgiveness prevents this and gives Satan a chance to make matters even worse (2 Corinthians 2:10-11).
- *Division*: Offended people are reckless and take the initiative to get even with others, no matter the interpersonal damage it might cause (Matthew 18:15-20).
- *Bitterness:* This is spiteful anger and loathing disappointment that produces sour, sarcastic, cynical, and unpleasant fruit (Hebrews 12:15).

Beside these negative consequences, we should forgive because:

- *Jesus forgave us:* Through sin, mankind offended God. However, God was the one who initiated forgiveness with us — even before we requested it (Matthew 26:28; Romans 5:8; Ephesians 4:32).
- *Forgiveness sets us free and sets others free:* Forgiveness absolves offenders of their wrong and halts revenge from taking place on either side. This is mentally, emotionally, spiritually, and physically liberating — especially in the long run (Matthew 18:26-27).
- *Forgiveness brings peace*: How often do grudges persist in families and other relationships longer than they have to? The only way to establish a truce and disarm the hostility is through forgiveness (Matthew 18:15).
- *Forgiveness is healthy:* Even health professionals admit that unforgiveness destroys our organs and shortens our lives. Is being unforgiving really worth the state of your health (Proverbs 14:30; 1 Corinthians 11:28-30)?
- *God commands it:* Following Jesus into his Kingdom means forgiving. God commands our obedience, even when it is difficult (Mark 11:25; Colossians 3:13).
- *When we forgive, we are forgiven:* If we want God to forgive our sins, we must forgive others for the wrong they have done to us (Matthew 6:14-15).

FORGIVENESS IS:

- *A decision of the will*: Forgiveness starts with a firm resolution that it is the correct thing to do. Nobody is forcing you; it is the result of your own consideration.
- *From the heart:* Forgiveness has to be sincere. Somewhere deep down, you must desire to offer that forgiveness toward your offender because God loves them despite their wrongdoing.
- *Not holding someone's wrong against him or her any more*: You release to God whatever desire you may have to seek your own justice. You establish God as your vindicator and trust that he will make things right. Going forward with the offender, you refuse any temptation to bring it back up (Romans 12:19).
- *Asking God to have mercy on the offender*: Love seeks the best for our enemies. Asking God to show our wrongdoer mercy and to not hold their trespass against them is the ultimate expression of Christ's love. When we reach this point, our heart is free from offense (Luke 23:34).

Forgiveness Is Not:

- *A feeling*: Forgiveness is an act of faith, not feeling. We will rarely ever feel like forgiving someone who has hurt us. Pay no attention to your feelings; we obey by faith and by conviction (2 Corinthians 5:7).
- *Forgetting*: A common misnomer is that true forgiveness means losing memory of what the person did to us. This is backed up with scripture from Isaiah 43:25 and Hebrews 8:12, where God says he will *remember our sins no more*.

However, *remember* in this case doesn't carry the idea *to forget* or *fail to recall*. It means that God will not take action against us because of our sin. Therefore, when we suspend our ability to get even, we are *forgetting* the transgressor's sin. Losing memory of how a person has offended us may happen supernaturally or it may happen over time, but don't wait until it does to decide to forgive.

- *Restoring the offender to the former position they had in your life:* God does not require you to give your offender the same place they once had in your life, especially if they broke your trust. Establishing new boundaries with an offender is a wise and necessary thing to do and is not contrary to what forgiveness is (Romans 12:21; Ephesians 4:2-3).

Below is a prayer asking the Lord to bring to your mind every person towards whom you have *hatred*, *bitterness*, *anger*, and *unforgiveness*. It includes those who have:

- *Hurt you.*
- *Offended you.*
- *Cheated you, stolen from you, or lied to you.*
- *Broken your heart.*
- *Taken advantage of you.*

Dear Heavenly Father, I confess that there have been those in my life who have done me wrong and have hurt me deeply. I am here because I desire to show them mercy and cancel their offences against me, as you have commanded. Please reveal to my mind every person whom I need to forgive and show me why I need to forgive them.

In return for my faith and obedience, I pray that you would show me mercy, set me free, and heal every part of me that is not whole due to unforgiveness. In Jesus' name, Amen.

In the space provided below, make a list of each person who has offended you significantly: those you believe are responsible for the pain you have in your soul. List their names, what they did, and how it made you feel. After, there is a space that says *Lies I Believed*. In this space, list anything you started believing about your identity that is contrary to God's Word. If you need more space, you may use the notes section in the back.

1. _____   _____
            (Name)   (Offense)

   _____   _____
       (How It Made Me Feel)   (Lies I Believed)

2. _____   _____
            (Name)   (Offense)

   _____   _____
       (How It Made Me Feel)   (Lies I Believed)

3. _____   _____
            (Name)   (Offense)

   _____   _____
       (How It Made Me Feel)   (Lies I Believed)

4. _____   _____
            (Name)   (Offense)

   _____   _____
       (How It Made Me Feel)   (Lies I Believed)

5. _____   _____
            (Name)   (Offense)

   _____   _____
       (How It Made Me Feel)   (Lies I Believed)

After you have completed your list, pray the following prayer to issue forgiveness. Forgive each person specifically and individually, and renounce each lie specifically and individually.

In the Name of Jesus, with my Heavenly Father as my witness, I forgive [*name*] for [*offense*] because it made me feel [*how it made me feel*]. I renounce the lie(s) that [*lies I have believed*] and I agree with what your Word says about me instead. I break any attachment that Satan has in my life because of the pain in my heart associated with this offense or because of the confusion it caused in my identity. I command every evil spirit to go from me now. In Jesus' name, Amen.

Lord, I ask that you have mercy on [*name*]. Lead them into finding forgiveness from you. I pray that they are able one day to stand before you cleansed from this offense and not have to experience punishment for it. From now unto eternity I will no longer hold this offense against [*name*]. Lord Jesus, thank you for setting me free.

In Christ

Lastly, it is important to replace every lie about your identity with the truth that God says about it. The most powerful way of doing this is to confess, daily, the scriptures that deal specifically with your new identity as a child of God. These scriptures point to your identity *in Christ*. Being *in Christ* simply means to be organically united to Christ, like the way a finger is united to a hand or the way a branch is connected to a vine. Just as you see a branch and a vine as one tree or a finger and a hand as one body, so God sees Christ and us as one relationship. Therefore, as Christ is holy, we are holy; as Christ is righteous, we are righteous. Get it? This is the blessing of salvation and has come through our faith in Christ's redemptive work. Christians need to learn these truths, especially right after deliverance.

Below is a list of these scriptures and a confession for you to say. It would benefit you greatly to study these scriptures and make these confessions part of your daily routine so that they go down deep into your heart and take root. Then you will see them producing all kinds of wonderful fruit in your identity and life.

BECAUSE I AM IN CHRIST...

God has decreed great things and marvelous things over my life. I am a recipient of the wonderful blessings of his kindness and grace. –Ephesians 1:3

God will bring to pass the blessings that he has declared over my life. I take confidence knowing that it is through his power that his promises to me will be fulfilled. He will see to it because he is faithful to me. –Philippians 1:6

I have been given tremendous authority over Satan, sin, and the Kingdom of Darkness. I have no need to be afraid of what the enemy might do because he is under my feet. –Ephesians 1:21; 2:6

I am God's masterpiece. As a skilled artisan forms his finest work, so God formed me. When God looks at me, he sees his very best work and rejoices. –Ephesians 2:10

I have found total fulfillment. There is no other experience needed to complete me. I have all I could ever need or want because of Christ. –Colossians 2:10

I have received a mind that is being filled by God's holy thoughts. I have values that are different from this present evil age. I am conscious and aware of the Kingdom of God, and I realize that this life and its glory is fading away. My mind is fixed on heavenly things. –1 Corinthians 2:16; –Colossians 2:3

I am more than a supreme victor! Never before has there been a victory as great as my victory over sin. Jesus has made me triumphant — a champion of champions! –Romans 8:37

I am safe from all accusations. There is no need to fear any condemnation from the former life. I have peace with God and am free from his wrath. –Romans 8:1

The love and favor that God has for Jesus has spilled over onto me. God favors me and loves me just as much as he loves Jesus. –Ephesians 1:6

I act like Christ each and every day. Through the help of the Holy Spirit, I constantly think like Christ. Therefore, people see the character of Jesus lived out through me. –Romans 13:14

PART 4
Generational Curses

GENERATIONAL CURSES ARE PERHAPS THE most misunderstood aspect of deliverance. Excessive non-New Testament teaching has been taught in the name of generational curses. Consequently, damage is done in the life and to the theology of believers. This damage leads to bad practice and unfruitful ministry, and in some cases, further oppression. Therefore, it's important to know what a generational curse is — especially in light of the work of Christ.

To begin, we must know a few things about disobedience to God, particularly what sin, transgression, and iniquity are. Notice:

I acknowledge my sin unto thee, and mine iniquity have I not hid. I said, I will confess my transgressions unto the Lord; and thou forgavest the iniquity of my sin. –Psalm 32:5

Though these words all refer to disobedience to God, they each have a different shade of meaning and reveal something important to us about wickedness.

- *Sin* means to miss the mark; doing the opposite of what is right before God; a shortcoming (Galatians 5:17; 1 John 5:17). It is anything that falls short of God's approval (Romans 3:23), whether knowingly or unknowingly.
- *Transgression* refers to presumptuous sin — intentionally sinning even though we know that we are wrong (Psalm 32:1). It is having knowledge of what is right and what is wrong and choosing to do wrong, in spite of that knowledge.
- *Iniquity* means a premeditated choice, continuing without repentance (Micah 2:1). It is not just sinning itself, but covering up that sin after it has been committed. It is a state of the heart. When David committed adultery with Bathsheba and got her pregnant, he tried to cover it up by having Uriah, her husband, executed (2 Samuel 11). When David finally repented, he asked God not only to forgive his sin but also to look deeper and forgive the premeditations of his heart that enabled him to commit that sin, that iniquity.

Iniquity is referred to as *lawlessness* in the New Testament (2 Peter 2:8). Peter uses it to describe the men of Sodom and Gomorrah who were defiant of God. This means that iniquity refers to a flagrant insubordination; holding God's laws in contempt, as worthless and beneath consideration.

Without repentance, iniquity leads to a reprobate mind (Romans 1:28). A reprobate mind is morally worthless thinking that God rejects. When a person's mind has become reprobate, their behavior will become twisted. That behavior will come to define who they are.

But reprobate behavior doesn't affect only the person behaving. It affects those closest to them ¾ —their families. Their reprobate thinking and behavior becomes a model for younger generations to follow. Their kids, grandchildren, and even great-grandchildren usually observe it and follow the same way. This is an inheritance of wickedness and is what is known as a generational curse. And it is called a curse because it will be the cause of lifelong suffering and failure, and it will block the prosperity of God's blessing.

How Do I Know If There Is Curse Active in My Life or Family?

- *Constant failure in spite of diligent work.*
- *Accident prone.*
- *Unexplained chronic sickness.*
- *Unceasing emotional and mental turmoil.*
- *Unending lack.*
- *Perpetual tragedies and unexpected deaths.*
- *Chaos and disorder in the family (arguing, divorce, abuse, miscarriages, domestic violence).*

Curses indicate the presence of demons. Just as smoke indicates fire and flies indicate trash, curses indicate demons. The same demons that have harassed your family in the past will harass you when you repeat your family's wickedness. These demons are known as *familiar spirits* (Leviticus 19:31).

The word *familiar* is from a Latin word that means a *household servant*. Evil spirits can be described as *household servants* because they hang around families and circulate the same evil. This explains why every generation might have a problem with the same sin or become addicted to the same thing. It also explains why certain abnormalities and illnesses keep appearing in the family line — wickedness and familiar spirits are still at work.

To find freedom from curses and the familiar spirits associated with them, all iniquity and wickedness must be confronted and dealt with through the work of Christ. It says in 1 Peter 1:18: *For you know that God paid a ransom to save you from the empty life you inherited from your ancestors.* Jesus cancelled the claims of iniquity over us and broke every curse when he redeemed us on the cross. Notice:

> *But Christ has rescued us from the curse pronounced by the law. When he was hung on the cross, he took upon himself the curse for our wrongdoing. For it is written in the Scriptures, "Cursed is everyone who is hung on a tree." Through Christ Jesus, God has blessed the Gentiles with the same blessing he promised to Abraham, so that we who are believers might receive the promised Holy Spirit through faith. –Galatians 3:13-14*

Therefore, our only option is to apply faith in the work of Christ and, at the same time, turn our back on our family's iniquity.

Our family's iniquity is what produces the curse. Iniquity is the root. Therefore, the Lord must show us what those iniquities are so that we can uproot them and walk free, even if we *haven't* repeated them. If we haven't repeated them, though we aren't guilty for them, there is still the possibility that they could someday ensnare us because they've been overlooked. It says in 1 Corinthians 10:12: *Therefore let him who thinks he stands take heed that he does not fall.*

Pray the following pray and ask the Holy Spirit to reveal to you all the iniquities of your ancestors:

> **Dear Heavenly Father, you are a loving, kind, and merciful God who desires to bless my family and me. You want us to live the abundant life. Your Word says that you show loving kindness to all of those who keep your commandments, but iniquity will be punished (Exodus 20:4-6). I desire to uproot all the iniquity in my family so that every curse can be broken and so that we can experience the fullness of your blessing. Holy Spirit, reveal to me where your mercy and grace is needed. I believe that through the blood of Jesus Christ my family and I can be free, both now and forever. In Jesus' name, Amen.**

Now that you have asked the Holy Spirit for his help, make a list of the iniquities in your family. They may go back farther than you can remember. Some examples are (but not limited to):

- *Addictions.*
- *Witchcraft/Occult.*

- *Hatred.*
- *Idolatry.*
- *Sins of the flesh.*
- *Dishonor.*
- *Racism.*
- *Rebellion.*
- *Twisted ways of thinking.*
- *National sin (wickedness commonly practiced in your family's country of origin).*
- *Gang involvement.*

Iniquities:

1. _____
2. _____
3. _____
4. _____
5. _____

After you have listed each iniquity, pray the following prayer and repent and renounce each one, specifically and individually.

> **Father, in the name of Jesus, I repent of and renounce [*iniquity*]. Cleanse me with the blood of Jesus and make me pure. I command every familiar spirit attached to this iniquity to go from my family and from me, now. I break any other attachment my family or I may have as the result of [*iniquity*]. I command any curse that has come as a result of [*iniquity*] to be broken and continue no further in my family's life or mine. In Jesus' name, Amen.**

THE MEANING OF YOUR NAME

The Scriptures teach us that our names have meaning (1 Samuel 25:3; Matthew 1:21). Often our given name is prophetic of our destiny. Because words have power, every time our given name is called, that meaning is spoken over us and into us. There are good names that release blessing, and there are bad names that release cursing.

Do you know the meaning of your given name? How about your middle, third, or fourth name if you have one? How about your surname: have you discovered what that means? A study and look into the etymology of your name can be enriching, insightful, and revealing. In the spaces below, write your names and their meanings (if you don't know their meanings, a Google search will be helpful). You should also include any nicknames you have been given.

Given Name_____   Meaning_____

Middle Name_____   Meaning_____

Surname_____   Meaning_____

Nickname(s)_____   Meaning_____

Not all names are hefty in significance or carry spiritual meaning. If your name means something neutral, there is no need for any concern or special prayer. However, if your name has a sinister or wicked meaning, you must renounce the meaning of your name and break off every curse that has been spoken over you when it's been called. Pray this prayer:

Heavenly Father, I thank you that you know me and who I am — apart from the name that was given to me. I renounce my name [*name*] and its meaning [*meaning*]. I pray that every curse that has come as a result of my name be broken off me, in the name of Jesus.

Lord, you said that you would set me apart and give me a new name (Revelation 2:17). From here on out, I declare that I am only known by you for who I truly am in Christ. No matter what people call me, those words will have no effect because I am hidden in Christ and am submitted solely to the purpose and destiny that you have for my life. In Jesus' name, Amen.

Now that you have renounced your name, refuse to identify with what that name means. People may still call you by that name and you may have to use that name the rest of your life. However, you have confronted its meaning and have put it under the blood of Jesus. You are free to see yourself the way God sees you: holy and pure.

Because you have prayed and consecrated your name to God, you can trust that evil words will have no power over you in the future. Never allow your identity to be determined by your name again. You are in Christ.

However, if you are still uncomfortable with your name after deliverance, you may want to consider changing it. There are some legal matters involved, but it might be worth it so you never have to hear that name again.

Prayer of Family Dedication

Father, in the name of Jesus, I thank you that you have set me apart from all the harmful generational influences of my ancestors. A great exchange has taken place: Jesus took my suffering and misery so that I could receive his blessing; he was beaten so that I could be whole; he was made sin so that I could be righteous. I have received this exchange in place of the ancestral curses of my family. Therefore, I have been rescued from the Kingdom of Darkness and am now part of the Kingdom of God (Colossians 1:13).

I no longer have an inheritance of wickedness. My inheritance is all of the spiritual blessings in Christ (Ephesians 1:3). This also means that I have cut off the work of iniquity from going any farther down into my family line. Instead, I fully expect to see your blessing at work.

I am so humble and so grateful, and I thank you, Lord. And now I pray for all those in my family who have not received what you have done for them. May the eyes of their understanding be enlightened (Ephesians 1:17-19). I pray that the god of this world (Satan) will be bound from deceiving them (2 Corinthians 4:4) so that they may receive Jesus and be free from the curses of iniquity. I stand and declare that all my family shall be saved (Acts 16:31). My parents and grandparents shall be saved, my siblings shall be saved, my spouse shall be saved, my kids shall be saved, and all the rest of my relatives shall be saved. The whole [*family surname*] family shall walk in the fullness of God's blessing. In Jesus' name, Amen.

PART 5
Sins of the Flesh

SINS OF THE FLESH (ALSO called *works of the flesh*, Galatians 5:19-21) are sinful actions contrary to God's design that humans indulge in to please their carnal appetites.

The Scriptures give us several lists that name many of these sinful actions (Mark 7:21-23; Romans 1:29-31; 1 Corinthians 6:9-10; Galatians 5:19-21; Revelation 21:8). Though these sins are numerous, they each can be sorted into at least one of five categories. They are:

- *Sins of Deceit*: Dishonest practices for the sake of personal advantage.
- *Sins of Excess:* Overindulgence and immoderation.
- *Sins of Misconduct*: Behavior that falls short of God's standard.
- *Sins of Omission*: Failing to do what God requires of us; failing to obey.
- *Sins of Sacrilege*: Twisting and perverting that which is holy or sacred.
- *Sins of Sexual Immorality*: Wicked and forbidden sexual behavior.

The *flesh* is a term that is used repeatedly in the New Testament and simply refers to the sinful nature (Romans 13:14; Galatians 5:17; Ephesians 2:3). The Word of God tells us to put to death this sinful nature (Galatians 5:24) and to *walk in the Spirit* (Galatians 5:16).

Walking in the Spirit means being obedient to the Holy Spirit; relying on the Holy Spirit to guide us in thought, word, and deed. It is the responsibility of every Christian to do this, daily.

When we walk in the Spirit, the flesh has no dominion over us (Romans 6:14). Obeying the Holy Spirit should be natural for us, as Christians, because the Holy Spirit dwells in us (Romans 8:9). Therefore, indulging in the sins of the flesh should be foreign to us because it is against our new nature (2 Corinthians 5:17). However, it is possible to sin.

Sin begins with temptation. Temptation is an incitement to behavior that doesn't please God. Temptation comes from Satan, the world, and the parts of our lives that are not yielded to God. If we don't rely on the help of the Holy Spirit and resist that temptation, we will commit sin. Sin damages our fellowship with God and hinders our faith. When we sin, we are to immediately confess that sin to God and ask for his forgiveness (1 John 1:9).

Unless you commit a very grave sin (Ezekiel 22:1-6), usually sinning once doesn't open up a door for a demon to enter into your life. We all make mistakes and God is merciful. God expects us to learn from those mistakes and to move forward (1 John 2:1).

However, habitually sinning will certainly create an entry point for evil spirits to enter our lives. Habitually committing sin is very dangerous because, in doing so, you are giving yourself over to that sin. When you give yourself over to it, that sin will become your master, and you will be its slave (John 8:34; Romans 6:20).

Once you are given over to a sin, it becomes an addiction — something you are unable to control without God's divine help. The reason you lose control is because a demon spirit has taken control and forces you against your will. If you don't receive deliverance, iniquity will form in you and you will likely pass it down into your family.

Sin has very serious consequences — spiritually, mentally, emotionally, physical, relationally, and even vocationally. We must treat sin like an enemy that wants to destroy our lives.

Below is a list of the sins of the flesh. Remember, they are not only transgressions of God's law, they are also entry points for demon spirits. Check each sin that you have participated in.

Sins of Deceit

☐ Cheating ☐ Exaggeration ☐ Lying ☐ Stealing ☐ Other_____

Sins of Excess

☐ Drunkenness ☐ Fearfulness ☐ Gluttony ☐ Greed ☐ Materialism ☐ Workaholism ☐ Worry
☐ Other_____

Sins of Misconduct

☐ Abortion ☐ Abuse ☐ Anger ☐ Animal Cruelty ☐ Cannibalism ☐ Divorce ☐ Envy ☐ Hatred
☐ Jealousy ☐ Fighting ☐ Gambling ☐ Gossip ☐ Manipulation ☐ Mockery ☐ Murder ☐ Pride
☐ Racism/Prejudice ☐ Revenge ☐ Rivalry ☐ Selfishness ☐ Strife ☐ Swearing ☐ Vandalism
☐ Vanity ☐ Other_____

Sins of Omission

☐ Apathy ☐ Disobeying Authority ☐ Disobeying God ☐ Disobeying Parents ☐ Laziness
☐ Neglecting Devotion to God (Prayer, Worship, Giving, etc.) ☐ Neglecting Responsibility
(Parent, Employee, Leader, etc.) ☐ Unforgiveness ☐ Other_____

Sins of Sacrilege

☐ Blasphemy ☐ Drug Use (Cocaine, Dope, Heroin, LSD, Nicotine, etc.) ☐ Idolatry ☐ Occult
☐ Voodoo ☐ Witchcraft ☐ Other_____

Sins of Sexual Immorality

☐ Adultery ☐ Bestiality ☐ Dirty Talking (Sexting, Virtual Sex, etc.) ☐ Exhibitionism ☐ Fetishism
☐ Fornication ☐ Frotteurism ☐ Homosexuality/Lesbianism ☐ Incest ☐ Incubi/Succubae
☐ Masturbation ☐ Molestation ☐ Orgies ☐ Pedophilia ☐ Pornography ☐ Prostitution
☐ Sadomasochism (S&M) ☐ Sodomy ☐ Transgenderism ☐ Transvestitism ☐ Voyeurism
☐ Other_____

After checking each box that pertains to you, pray the following prayer of repentance and renounce each sin specifically and individually:

> **Dear Heavenly Father, I come to you seeking your mercy and your forgiveness. I have committed the sin of [*sin*] and have given Satan an entry point into my life. I repent for each time I have committed the sin of [*sin*] and I renounce it totally and completely.**
>
> **I ask you to make me clean, pure, and holy. I command every spirit that has gained access into my life as the result of [*sin*] to come out, in the name of Jesus. Come out of my mind. Come out of my emotions. Come out of my body. Go from me now. I break every attachment to every devil.**
>
> **Now, Lord Jesus, I ask you to fill me fresh with your Holy Spirit because I am a clean vessel. In Jesus' name, Amen.**

Dealing With Sexual Immorality and Soul Ties

The Scriptures make a special point of warning us of the dangers associated with sexual immorality. Notice:

> *Or do you not know that the one who joins himself to a prostitute is one body with her? For He says, "The two shall become one flesh." But the one who joins himself to the Lord is one spirit with Him. Flee immorality. Every other sin that a man commits is outside the body, but the immoral man sins against his own body. Or do you not know that your body is a temple of the Holy Spirit who is in you, whom you have from God, and that you are not your own? For you have been bought with a price: therefore glorify God in your body.*
> *–1 Corinthians 6:16-20*

Sexual immorality differs from other sins for several reasons:

- *We defile our body*: No sin is as depraved as sexual sin. Sexual sin degrades the offender and makes them unclean (1 Corinthians 6:18).
- *It stains our life with disgrace:* No other sin is stigmatized with dishonor and shame the way sexual sin is (Proverbs 6:32-33).
- *We become joined to our sexual partner (soul ties):* Sexual intercourse is not an inconsequential act. Rather, it is an enduring bond that unites two partners in an intimate way. Scripture tells us that sex makes us one with our partner (1 Corinthians 6:16). In

fact, it was believed in New Testament times that having sex with a temple prostitute would unite you to the gods they serve.

Needless to say, the bond of sex is extremely powerful. When reserved for marriage, it bonds the married couple in a divine way; and that bond is never broken. However, when couples have sex outside of marriage, they create a bond that is broken when the relationship ends. Their lives become fragmented because their mate moves on with pieces of them. Therefore, not only does each party have a void because their mate took something, they also are stuck with a piece of their mate. This means they are still *attached*. This is a *soul-tie* — a spiritual, emotional, mental, or physical attachment that connects you to someone else.

A soul-tie:

- *Disables you from moving on from your past relationship(s).*
- *Produces irrational thinking.*
- *Produces unhealthy attraction.*
- *Creates lack of good judgment.*
- *Causes immaturity in relationships.*

Soul-ties can be broken through prayer, repentance, and renunciation. For each person with whom you have had sexual intercourse with or engaged in foreplay with (including all forms of non-penetrative sex: oral, anal, and heavy petting), pray the following prayer for each, specifically and individually. (If you eventually married the person, you must still pray because you created a bond at the wrong time, and God cannot bless that.) Should you need to make a list, use the notes section in the back.

> **Dear Heavenly Father, I repent for [*sexual sin*] with [*name of partner*]. I renounce this sin and every single soul-tie that I have created with them, spiritually, emotionally, mentally, and physically. I ask that you break it now. In Jesus' name, Amen.**

Dealing With Murder (Including Abortion)

Murder is another sin that Scripture points out with special effort because of its seriousness. Murder is unlawfully taking another human being's life. It is often done out of hate, ill will, and malice. Included in murder is abortion. Abortion is the deliberate termination of a human fetus. This is murder because life begins at conception (Jeremiah 1:5; Psalm 139:13, 16).

Not only is murder an offense to the victim, murder is an offense to the victim's posterity (Genesis 4:10). By taking a life, you cut off future generations of people who would have come if the victim had remained alive.

Nevertheless, God is loving and will forgive murder. The work of Christ has satisfied the divine demands of justice and retribution and has brought us reconciliation and peace with God (Hebrews 12:24).

If you have committed murder, it is important to repent specifically and individually for each person that you have killed. After, ask God to shower his blessing upon that person's family for having cut off some of its posterity.

> **Dear Heavenly Father, I confess to you that I have murdered [*name*]. I am so sorry and am in need of your mercy. Forgive me, Lord. I renounce this as sin and pray that every demonic influence involved in this murder be broken off of my life. Lord, I can never show resolution to [*name*]'s family. Only you can bless them for my actions against them. Extend your grace to them. In Jesus' name, Amen.**

If you have committed abortion, God loves you. You can trust that God has taken your baby to heaven. The best evidence that babies go to heaven is in 2 Samuel 12:23. David's baby son had died. Knowing that he cannot bring him back from the dead, David says, *I shall go to him, but he shall not return to me.* David believed he would be with his child in heaven one day.

Though each child is conceived with a sinful nature (Psalm 51:5), a baby never has the opportunity to willfully sin (especially an unborn baby). Without doubt we can trust that God is full of goodness and mercy (Psalm 23:6) and somehow he applies the work of Christ so that he can bring those children home to heaven with him. You will see your child again one day, and God's love will reconcile you together. Until that time, it is important to ask God for mercy and grace to continue running your race, free from the guilt and shame from which Christ has delivered you.

Pray the following prayer specifically and individually for each child that you have aborted. (If that child did not have a name, use the year in which the abortion was committed to refer to them.)

> **Dear Heavenly Father, I am so deeply sorrowful for having an abortion. I confess it was murder. Please forgive me for aborting [*name*]. I trust that they are with you in heaven. Please heal me from my guilt, shame, and any and all disorder**

that has come upon my life because of this abortion. May every demonic influence involved in this abortion be broken off my life. I ask you now, Lord, to extend to me mercy and grace so that I can continue to run the race that you have marked out for me (Hebrews 12:1). In Jesus' name, Amen.

Ungodly Tattoos

While there is no specific instruction in the New Testament concerning tattoos, we are commanded to treat our bodies as the temple of God (1 Corinthians 6:19). This means treating our body as though it is God's property. Fulfilling this means keeping wickedness from defiling it.

In the Old Testament, God forbade his people from marking their bodies with the evil images and designs of idols and pagan deities. A tattoo of an idol meant that the individual was a servant to that idol and would come under the influence of the spirit behind that idol. This was an outrage to God. We must obey God and keep our bodies free from markings of evil and even questionable designs. If not, it is possible evil spirits represented by the marks we take can influence us.

Tattoos are notorious for representing death (skulls, snakes, demons, spiders), idolatry (tikis, totems, mythology), spiritualism (sayings from exotic religions), and associations (clubs, relationships, pacts, cults). Nothing should go on our bodies that Jesus has overcome: death, demons, false religion, etc.

Furthermore, nothing should go on our bodies that binds us to anything other than Christ. We belong to him and cannot be divided in whom we serve (Matthew 6:24). In fact, God has set his seal of ownership on us (2 Corinthians 1:22) to denote we belong to him. That should be enough. Marking your bodies contrariwise is rebellion and is asking for trouble.

If you have any tattoos on your body that represents anything against the holiness of God, pray the following prayer. Repent for and renounce every tattoo specifically and individually.

Heavenly Father, I take your words and your instructions seriously. You have told me not to mark my body with wickedness or put anything on my body that makes me servant to anything besides you. I repent for getting [*tattoo*]. I renounce it and anything it binds me to. I ask you to break every attachment it binds me to. Thank you for your mercy and grace. I declare I belong totally and completely to you. In Jesus' name, Amen.

Prayer of Personal Holiness

Heavenly Father, I come before you in Jesus' name. You have told us that you want us to be holy because you are holy (1 Peter 1:16). You have given me a distinct standard whereby I should live my life; a standard that separates me from the world and reveals that I belong to you. This is this standard that I am striving for by the power of your Holy Spirit — it is my goal and my heart's desire.

Therefore, I declare that I am done with the flesh and its passions and desires. Sin does not have dominion over me. My old ways of behaving are done, over with and finished. My past is dead and no longer defines who I am. I declare every part of me that I have sinned with now belongs to you. My body belongs to you. My mind belongs to you. My soul and emotions belong to you. And my spirit and will belong to you.

I am no longer unclean, impure, dirty, or flawed. I am the righteousness of God because I am in Christ Jesus (2 Corinthians 5:21). Because Jesus Christ dwells in me, I couldn't be anymore unacceptable to God. Therefore, I accept myself. In Jesus' name, Amen.

PART 6
Mental and Emotional Issues

How you behave always affects your mind. And what goes on in your mind always affects the way you feel. Sinful behavior takes a toll on its participants and this is one of the reasons God forbids it. Humans were not created for sin; we are not compatible with it. We were created in God's image; created for holiness (Genesis 1:27; Ephesians 4:24). Holiness brings us an abundant life (John 10:10) but sin brings death (Romans 3:23). This is why we are to strive for holiness and avoid sin (1 Peter 1:16).

To specifically understand why sin affects us so drastically, we must first understand how we are made. Humans *are* a spirit, *possess* a soul, and *live* in a body (1 Thessalonians 5:23; Hebrews 4:12). Notice:

- *Spirit:* The part of us that lives eternally, has fellowship with God, and is recreated when we are born again (2 Corinthians 5:17).
- *Soul:* The part of us that feels, including our emotions (Psalm 35:9).
- *Body:* Our physical man; the part of us that interacts in the physical world through its five senses (1 Corinthians 6:19).

While there are three divisions that make up who we are, it is important to note that they do not work independently of one another. They all work as a perfectly integrated and seamless unit.[3] They are all valuable, precious, and should be consecrated to God.

It is challenging to say which of the three the mind belongs to. However, it really doesn't matter. What is important to know is that the mind is inseparably joined with them. This means that they are constant influences on one another. In other words, you can't sin in your thinking without affecting the way you feel. You cannot defile your body without affecting the way you think. You can't accept lousy emotions without it being detrimental to your health.

---

3 Chris Palmer. *Living as a Spirit: Hearing the Voice of God On Purpose* (Bloomington, IN: Westbow Press, 2014), 106.

Sinning is like uploading a virus onto a computer; no matter where it enters, it makes its way through all of the computer's systems and destroys them.

In light of this, many of the mental and emotional problems that have become so prevalent today are due to the constant practice of sin. Have you noticed that there is an increase in people who take anti-depressants, especially among young people? Isn't it obvious that mental disorders have become more common? This is connected to the fact that sin has increased. Notice:

Because lawlessness is increased, most people's love will grow cold. —Matthew 24:12

But mark this: There will be terrible times in the last days. People will be lovers of themselves, lovers of money, boastful, proud, abusive, disobedient to their parents, ungrateful, unholy, without love, unforgiving, slanderous, without self-control, brutal, not lovers of the good, treacherous, rash, conceited, lovers of pleasure rather than lovers of God—having a form of godliness but denying its power... Just as Jannes and Jambres opposed Moses, so also these teachers oppose the truth. They are men of depraved minds, who, as far as the faith is concerned, are rejected. —2 Timothy 3:1-5, 8

The end times are connected to an increase in sin, which results in cold-heartedness and depravity of mind. Depraved means to be led astray, morally decayed, and ruined. It describes something defective and deficient. When a person sins, it is because their minds are led astray. If they continue sinning and don't repent, their thinking will become decayed and their mind will become defective.

Though some mental and emotional issues are the result of physiological issues that require physical healing, many are simply the manifestation of a depraved mind.

Through deliverance, God desires to mend your broken mind from the debilitating effects of sin. Below is a list of issues that are the common result of a depraved mind. If you have a history of these or have struggled with them, God loves you. They do not define who you are because you are now new in Christ. However, you must confront them and ask God to heal you. Check each issue that you have battled.

> ### Mental and Emotional Issues
>
> ☐ ADHD ☐ Anorexia Nervosa ☐ Antisocial Personality Disorder ☐ Binge Eating Disorder ☐ Bipolar Disorder ☐ Bulimia Nervosa ☐ Borderline Personality Disorder ☐ Catatonia ☐ Compulsive Buying ☐ Chemical Dependencies ☐ Depersonalization Disorder ☐ Depression ☐ Dissociative Amnesia ☐ Fascination with Death ☐ Erotomania ☐ Fregoli Delusion ☐ Generalized Anxiety Disorder ☐ Hypochondria ☐ Intermittent Explosive Disorder ☐ Insomnia ☐ Kleptomania ☐ Klüver-Bucy Syndrome ☐ Low Self-Esteem ☐ Manic Episode ☐ Multiple Personality Disorder ☐ Narcissistic Personality Disorder ☐ Nightmares/Night Terrors ☐ Obsessive Compulsive Disorder (OCD) ☐ Panic Disorder ☐ Paranoia ☐ Perfectionism ☐ Psychosis ☐ Pyromania ☐ Post-Traumatic Stress Disorder (PTSD) ☐ Same-sex Attraction ☐ Schizoaffective Disorder ☐ Schizophrenia ☐ Self-harm ☐ Social Anxiety Disorder Substance Abuse (Drugs, Alcoholism, etc.) ☐ Suicidal Desires and Thoughts ☐ Other_____
>
> ☐ Phobias_____ _____ _____

After checking each box that pertains to you, pray the following prayer for each issue specifically and individually. Ask God to heal you and to mend your broken mind and emotions. You can have faith that God will heal you because:

- *God is a merciful God and shows compassion to those who love him* (Deuteronomy 7:9).
- *Jesus came to destroy the works of the devil, and that includes your issue(s)* (1 John 3:8).

Heavenly Father, I come to you now, asking for your mercy. Jesus came to destroy the works of Satan and sin. This includes the destruction that they have caused in my life. Lord Jesus, I place my faith in you. Heal me from [*issue*]. Deliver me totally and completely. I command any evil spirit causing this issue to go from me now. I thank you, Lord, that your delivering power is working in my life. In Jesus' name, Amen.

Traumatic Events and Anger at God

Experiencing or witnessing traumatic events can cause serious mental and emotional turmoil. Some of these events include:

- *War.*
- *Fatal or serious accidents.*
- *Death of a loved one.*
- *Destruction and chaos.*

Not only can these cause a wide variety of mental and emotional problems, they can cause spiritual problems such as:

- *Anger toward God.*
- *Anger toward God's representatives.*
- *Disbelief in God.*
- *Spiritual confusion.*
- *Spiritual apathy and disinterest.*
- *Reckless behavior.*

While we will not always know why certain things happen, we must trust Jesus and use our faith in him to resolve what we do not quite understand as humans. God is the source of life and in him there is no darkness at all (1 John 1:5). God is love (1 John 4:8) and he is our solution and not our problem. Accepting this is the first step toward resolving any anger and confusion toward him.

If you have anger toward God or any other spiritual problem because of a traumatic event that you have experienced or witnessed, pray the following prayer below specifically and individually for each event. Should you need to make a list, use the notes section in the back.

Heavenly Father, I come before you now and I admit to you that I am angry and confused because of [*event*]. I repent for thinking that you are the cause of it. I know that is not the truth. You are love and you would never do anything to hurt me. Forgive me for being angry at you. Heal my emotional wounds, my confusion, and my doubts about you.

I place my faith and my confidence in you, Jesus. I know that one day it will make sense. But until that day, I trust in you. In Jesus' name, Amen.

LIES OF SATAN

The Scriptures tell us that Satan is the father of lies (John 8:44) and goes about deceiving the whole world (Revelation 12:9). Satan uses trickery to manipulate our identity and make us believe that we are something that we are not. Our identity in Christ is the most important thing we have in order to maintain the mind of Christ (1 Corinthians 2:16) and our mental well-being. This is why the enemy attacks us in the mind.

God's Word tells us to put on the full armor of God so that we might stand against the assaults of Satan (Ephesians 6:10). These are largely mental assaults that come through deception

(Ephesians 6:16). If we fail to stand in the truth of God's Word, we will believe these lies and it will affect our behavior and our fellowship with God.

Below, mark each lie that you have believed about yourself that has affected your identity.

1. _____

2. _____

3. _____

4. _____

5. _____

After you have listed each lie, pray the following prayer for each lie specifically and individually.

Heavenly Father, I repent for believing [*lie*]. This is a deception of the enemy. You have not created me this way. I renounce this lie and any effect it has had on my life spiritually, emotionally, mentally, and physically. I command every evil spirit associated with it to go now. In Jesus' name, Amen.

Declaration of Renewal

In the name of Jesus, I declare that I am blessed of God. A complete renewal is taking place in my mind, emotions, and my body. The effects of sin have been broken. Whatever burden I once carried, I no longer carry because Christ has taken it from me. Whatever modern medicine was unable to do to heal me, Jesus did it on the cross; he has destroyed the power of sin and the works of the devil. Therefore, a restoration has taken place in me.

I declare that I have the mind of Christ (1 Corinthians 2:16). Because of this, the peace of God is coming over my life — the peace that passes all understanding (Philippians 4:7). A quietness is overtaking my mind. A rest is happening in my soul. And I owe it to the mercy of God that has come through Christ Jesus. In Jesus' name, Amen.

PART 7
Pride and Rebellion

THE ORIGINAL SIN WAS PRIDE. Pride means to be excessively full of yourself; to be blind with conceit; to be arrogantly superior to others. It was Lucifer who committed this sin (Isaiah 14:12-17).

Lucifer was a guardian angel and most likely, the highest created angel (Ezekiel 28:12-14). Because of his beauty, Lucifer became arrogant. His thinking became so skewed with pride that he decided that he would try exalt and enthrone himself above God (1 Timothy 3:6; Revelation 12:4). This led to a rebellion that caused his downfall.

Lucifer is now the prince of the power of the air (Ephesians 2:2), the god of this world (2 Corinthians 4:4), and the adversary of mankind. In fact, that is what his new name, *Satan*, means — *adversary* (Acts 26:18). Though he was defeated by God, Satan continues his proud rebellion by seeking to gain the worship of mankind while opposing the Kingdom of God.

This brief history of Satan teaches us that pride leads to rebellion. Rebellion is resisting authority; and, in this case, God's authority and those whom God has set in authority. When we rebel, we are acting in pride as if our way is higher than God's. The Scriptures teach that pride and rebellion come before a great fall, just as it did for Satan. Notice:

Pride goes before destruction, and haughtiness before a fall. –Proverbs 16:18

REBELLION AGAINST AUTHORITY

It is important to repent for the areas of our lives where we have rebelled against law and authority. God has placed authority in our lives to help us, cover us, protect us, and guide us. All authority is an extension of God's authority and we must treat it that way and honor it (Romans 13:1-7). The only time we can disobey authority is when authority becomes wicked and demands disobedience to God.

Below are extensions of authority that we commonly interact with, daily, throughout our lives. Check off each one that you have been rebellious toward.

Authority

- ☐ God
- ☐ Parents
- ☐ Spouse
- ☐ Government (Offices, Officials, Organizations, Departments)
- ☐ Pastors and Church Leadership
- ☐ Civil Authority (Police, Firemen, Public Servants)
- ☐ Teachers/Coaches
- ☐ Employers
- ☐ Other_____

After checking each box that pertains to you, pray the following prayer of repentance and renounce each area specifically and individually.

Dear Heavenly Father, you say in your Word that rebellion is wicked (1 Samuel 15:23). I repent for rebelling against [*authority*]. I renounce this rebellion. I desire to be obedient and from here on out I will treat [*authority*] with honor. In Jesus' name, Amen.

PRIDE

Repeated rebellion indicates a root of pride. When we consider where we have rebelled, we will find proud thinking. God despises the proud (James 4:16). This means that he opposes their plans. This is because God is against anyone who tries to steal his glory. All glory belongs to God alone and he will not share that glory with anyone else (Isaiah 42:8).

Pride is an attempt to steal what belongs to God; it is feeling entitled to what only God deserves. When we continue in pride, we will do things our own way and not God's way — rebellion. This is sure to lead to punishment and a difficult life (Proverbs 16:5).

However, the Scriptures tell us that when we humble ourselves and give glory to God, he gives us grace (James 4:6). This means that he gets involved in our plans and helps us bring them to pass.

In the list below, there are some common proud ways of thinking. Check each box that pertains to you. If there are other proud thoughts that commonly drive your behavior, list them in the spaces provided.

Common Proud Thoughts

- ☐ I am the cause of my own success.
- ☐ I can do it on my own; I don't need anyone's help, not even God's.
- ☐ I have everything I want, why do I need God?
- ☐ I am the best; nobody is better than I am.
- ☐ I am not wrong; other people are wrong.
- ☐ My needs are more important than others.
- ☐ I deserve more credit than I get.
- ☐ I am more special than others.
- ☐ I am too busy for God and others.
- ☐ People should listen to me more.
- ☐ I deserve what they have.
- ☐ Other_____

After you have checked each box that pertains to you, pray the following prayer of repentance and renounce each thought specifically and individually.

Heavenly Father, you said that pride comes before destruction and haughtiness comes before a fall. I repent for all of my pride and for thinking [*proud thought*]. I renounce this root of thinking in my life. I willingly humble myself before you and choose to live my life dependent upon your grace.

In everything I do, I will give you all of the glory and honor. You are the reason I am who I am. In Jesus' name, Amen.

YIELD TO GOD

Every area of life should be yielded to God. That means, at any time and for any reason, God should be able to direct us concerning that area and have our immediate obedience — no matter how impossible the challenge might seem. When we live with this kind of humility and submission toward God, we will reap a tremendous blessing and leave behind a marvelous inheritance and a lasting legacy (Psalm 112).

Furthermore, since our accomplishments are by the grace of God, we should give God all the glory for the success we have in these areas.

Below is a list of the most precious areas of our lives. Examine them. If you have not submitted yourself to God or if you have failed to give God glory for your success in these areas, check the box beside them.

Precious Areas of Life

- ☐ Marriage
- ☐ Family
- ☐ Relationships
- ☐ Education
- ☐ Career
- ☐ Income
- ☐ Achievements
- ☐ Ministry
- ☐ Other_____

After you have checked each box that pertains to you, pray the following prayer of repentance and renounce pride in each area specifically and individually. Then, yield each area to God in humility.

> **Dear Heavenly Father, I thank you for all the success that I have experienced in [*area of life*]. I repent for not having acknowledged you as the source of that success. I renounce this pride. Also, I am sorry for failing to yield myself to you in [*area of life*]. I willingly submit this area of my life to you now. You, Lord, now**

have complete control. Help me to continue to achieve and succeed so that I may leave behind a marvelous inheritance and lasting legacy to those who come after me. In Jesus' name, Amen.

TELLING GOD *NO* AND DEALING WITH REGRET

Perhaps the biggest mistake we can make in life is to tell God *no* when he asks us to do something. The result is deep regret and missing out on the blessings of obedience. Have you ever told God no? Has it caused deep regret? Though you may never get to partake in blessing that could have come if you had obeyed, you don't have to hang on to your regret the rest of your life. God is merciful and wants to extend his love to you and deliver you from the torment of regret.

In the spaces below, write where you have told God *no*. Next to it, write down the regret that you are holding onto because of it.

1. _____   _____
   (Where You Told God No)   (Regret)

2. _____   _____
   (Where You Told God No)   (Regret)

3. _____   _____
   (Where You Told God No)   (Regret)

After you have made your list, pray the following prayer of repentance. Renounce your pride and rebellion. Then ask God to set you free from regret and heal you from your pain.

Dear Heavenly Father, I am so sorry for telling you no when [*where you told God no*]. My pride and rebellion has caused me bitter pain and regret. I wish I could go back and have another chance, but I will never have that. So I repent and ask you for your mercy and your grace. I renounce my disobedience. Please remove the tormenting regret I am carrying and heal me from my pain. Give me your peace. I pray that you would bless all those affected by my disobedience.

From here on out, I will say yes to whatever you ask from me. In Jesus' name, Amen.

Prayer of Humility and Obedience

Heavenly Father, you tell us to humble ourselves in your sight and that, in return, you will lift us up (James 4:10). Lord, I am doing that right now. I declare that I am your conscious servant. Nothing in my life is my own; it all belongs to you. Everything I have is because of you, and I am just your steward.

From this point forward I will look at myself as equal with every person, and not simply as an equal, but as their servant. You said that the first will come last and the last will come first (Matthew 20:16). I want to serve with the same heart with which you served mankind. Fill me with that heart now, Lord. As a result of having a humble servant's heart, I will never tell you no when you ask me to do anything. Your ways are higher than mine (Isaiah 55:9). Therefore, I will do what you ask with joy and expectation, knowing that there is a blessing that comes with my unreserved obedience. It is a joy to be your servant, Lord. Your yoke is easy and your burden is light (Matthew 11:30). In Jesus' name, Amen.

PART 8

Receive the Baptism in the Holy Spirit

GOD'S WORD TELLS US THAT we must be filled totally with the Holy Spirit after we have been delivered. Otherwise, we will lose our deliverance. Notice what Jesus taught:

When an evil spirit leaves a person, it goes into the desert, seeking rest but finding none. Then it says, 'I will return to the person I came from.' So it returns and finds its former home empty, swept, and in order. Then the spirit finds seven other spirits more evil than itself, and they all enter the person and live there. And so that person is worse off than before. –Matthew 12:43-45

You can expect that the enemy will come back to see if he is welcome in your life again (Ephesians 6:11). And if he finds you habitually sinning, he will accept that as an invite in. And not only will he come back into your life, he will invite other demons as well. Those who have fallen back into sin often acknowledge that their second bout with their problem was much worse than the first. This is due to the increase in demonic presence.

God's Word warns us to resist the devil. This is our duty as soldiers of Christ. Notice:

- *So that Satan will not outsmart us. For we are familiar with his evil schemes. –2 Corinthians 2:11*
- *Put on all of God's armor so that you will be able to stand firm against all strategies of the devil. –Ephesians 6:11*
- *So humble yourselves before God. Resist the devil, and he will flee from you. –James 4:7*
- *Stay alert! Watch out for your great enemy, the devil. He prowls around like a roaring lion, looking for someone to devour. Stand firm against him, and be strong in your faith. –1 Peter 5:8-9a*

These four verses emphasize the need to be prepared to resist giving Satan a place in our life. At any time he could try to come and take ground. So we must be prepared, lest we fall. Notice:

If you think you are standing strong, be careful not to fall. –1 Corinthians 10:12

But we do not need to be afraid! These verses were not written to make us anxious; they were written to turn our faith to God who supplies all of our needs according to his glorious riches in Christ (Philippians 4:19). Through his plan in Christ, God has defeated Satan and made every provision for our victory. As long as we are focused on what God tells us to do, we always triumph (1 Corinthians 15:57).

One of the essential things that God tells us to do to is to be filled with his Spirit (Ephesians 5:18-19). And there are two types of fillings spoken of in Scripture to be experienced. They are:

- *The Indwelling Spirit*: This is the filling of the Spirit that initiates the believer into the body of Christ. This comes at salvation and is the Holy Spirit living inside every one that believes. All Christians have this—there is no such thing as a Christian who does not have the Holy Spirit within (1 Corinthians 12:3; 1 Timothy 6:16; 2 Timothy 1:14).
- *The Baptism in the Holy Spirit*: This is a baptism available to all believers and every servant of God. This baptism comes after salvation and is a spiritual power beyond our experience at salvation. Though not necessary for salvation, it is commanded by Jesus to have (Luke 24:49; Acts 1:8).

Facts About the Baptism in the Holy Spirit

Because you have received Jesus Christ as your Lord and Savior, you have the indwelling Holy Spirit within. However, depending on your experience with the Holy Spirit after conversion, you may or may not have been baptized in the Holy Spirit.

Before you leave your deliverance session, it is imperative for you to have this experience so that you have all the power God has made available to you to resist the enemy. Here are some things you should know that will help you to receive it.

- *The Baptism in the Holy Spirit is necessary for New Testament power*: Christians that have *not* been baptized in the Spirit often share about a wonderful experience at salvation. However, they often admit to having a lack of boldness and ministerial power. Such Christians should follow the apostle Paul's own experience: *after* his conversion, he received the Baptism in the Spirit. This enabled him to successfully fulfill all that God had in store for him (Acts 9:17).

- *The Baptism in the Holy Spirit was promised to us by the Father*: This experience was what Joel prophesied in Joel 2:28-32 and what was released to the world in Acts 2.
- *The Baptism of the Holy Spirit is where the early church got its ministry power*: Throughout the book of Acts, early Christians received the Spirit and went on to demonstrate the power of the resurrected Christ and to trample the works of Satan (Acts 10:44-48; Acts 19:1-5).
- *The Baptism of the Holy Spirit is accompanied with other tongues*: Each time a believer was baptized in the Spirit in the book of Acts, it was accompanied with other tongues not previously learned by the recipient. This is still the case today. In fact, the Apostle Paul said he desired all Christians to speak with tongues (1 Corinthians 14:5). Also, he constantly used tongues as a means of prayer (1 Corinthians 14:18).

Speaking and praying in tongues will be a constant source of edification to you. It will help you to thwart the onslaughts of Satan and to overcome and stand firm in obedience to God.

How to Receive the Baptism in the Holy Spirit

The Baptism in the Holy Spirit is received the same way anything else is received from God: by faith. God has made this experience available to us by his love and his grace. Therefore, it is ours for the taking. Here are some things to help you before you ask the Lord for it:

- *It is a gift and cannot be earned:* No matter how good or how bad you have lived your life, you don't deserve this experience. But God has given it to you anyway. Though it is free to you, Christ paid a great price for you to have it. When you accept, you are getting what Christ paid for you to have (Acts 2:38). So receive!
- *You must hunger and desire it:* God never honors us with what we don't desire. Desire is the beginning of seeking and seeking leads to finding (Matthew 7:7-8). If your heart does not reach for the Baptism in the Holy Spirit, you simply won't receive it. However, if you heart desires it, it will be yours.
- *Believe you receive when you ask:* Jesus taught us to believe that we receive when we pray (Mark 11:22-24). This means to expect that you have what you have asked for, the moment you ask for it. This is faith. Expect it now!
- *The Holy Spirit is transmitted through the laying on of hands:* There are five instances in the book of Acts where people receive the Baptism in the Holy Spirit. In three of those instances, the individuals received when hands were laid on them (Acts 8:14-17; Acts 9:17; Acts 19:1-6).

If you going through deliverance with a counselor, allow them to lay hands on you and pray for you to receive. If you are taking yourself through deliverance, you may receive it without laying on of hands (Acts 2:1-4; Acts 10:44-46).

What You Can Expect After Receiving the Baptism in the Holy Spirit

- *Signs and wonders when you minister, pray, and preach the Gospel.*
- *More boldness.*
- *An increased desire for personal holiness.*
- *A greater love for Jesus.*
- *A consuming desire to see the Kingdom of God come in its fullness.*
- *A better understanding of spiritual things, including God's Word.*
- *Praying in tongues.*
- *A stronger ability to resist temptation.*

Prayer to Receive the Baptism in the Holy Spirit

Dear Heavenly Father, I come before you now with faith and expectation. You have poured out your Spirit upon all flesh, including me. Today I want to receive this. I thank you that the baptism in the Holy Spirit is a gift for all of those who are in Christ Jesus. You said that I would receive power when the Spirit has come upon me. I look forward to walking in a new dimension of power and authority over the works of the enemy.

So I ask you, Lord Jesus, to baptize me in the Holy Spirit and in fire, right now. Fill me to overflowing. May rivers of living water flow out of my belly (John 7:37-38). May I be your holy mouthpiece from this day forward. May I walk in signs and wonders and demonstrate your soon coming, unshakeable Kingdom. In Jesus' name, Amen.

After you have prayed that prayer, expect that you can speak and pray in tongues. Open your mouth and worship and exalt God. As you do so, the Holy Spirit will fill your mouth with heavenly language.

Maintaining Your Deliverance

Jesus said, *And you will know the truth, and the truth will set you free* (John 8:32). He also said, *So if the Son sets you free, you are truly free* (John 8:36).

God delights in your freedom and is jubilant that you have overcome through the power of his grace. As you go forward in your newly found liberty, there are a few things that you can do to be sure that you maintain what God has done in your life. Deliverance is not a one-time session, it is a lifestyle. The following points will help you to live that lifestyle.

- *Schedule a follow-up appointment with your counselor:* A follow-up appointment will give you and your counselor a sense of how you have done over a short period of time. It will give you the opportunity to reinforce truths about your identity in Christ, dispel uncertainties, and encourage you to stay steadfast in holiness. You should aim to make your follow up appointment anywhere from 4-8 weeks after your deliverance session.
- *Get rid of any evil possessions:* Don't forget to go home and throw everything in the trash that brings evil into your life or your family's life. This might even mean deleting software such as apps, mp3 files, etc. Don't hesitate to destroy something because it cost you money. Your freedom is more valuable than the money you spent for that thing. And don't give it away to someone else. You will be just setting them up to be in bondage. God will bless your decision to destroy it completely.
- *Find accountability:* We cannot run the race of holiness alone; we need faithful brothers and sisters to observe our behavior and keep us answerable. Your pastor won't often have the ability to keep everyone accountable in the church. Therefore, he should have delegated mentors and discipleship leaders around the church whose sole purpose is your accountability. These are individuals who are not too familiar with you and, as a result, won't let you off the hook easily. Honor these people and let them speak into your life. In return, you will grow.

- *Go to church:* If you are not around God's Word or God's people consistently, your walk with God will suffer. In return, you might start to give ground to the devil. Going to church keeps your faith fresh and alive. Hearing a fresh word from God taught by anointed teachers every week will grow you very quickly (Hebrews 10:25).
- *Maintain a disciplined devotional life:* Daily prayer by the help of the Spirit and meditating the Word of God is the only way for you to renew your mind. Remember, mind renewal is the biggest part of deliverance. Therefore, meditating and praying over God's Word will keep you delivered (Joshua 1:8).
- *Break ungodly friendships:* Nothing will undo your progress quicker than poor influences. We become the company we keep. For the sake of maintaining your freedom, get rid of your sinful friends and establish godly friendships (1 Corinthians 15:33). Remember, eagles fly with eagles. Don't worry about ministering to them: either God will find someone else to minister to them or he will use you when you have become more solid in your relationship with the Lord. Right now your primary concern needs to be yourself.
- *Remember that you are still growing:* Nobody is perfect. When you leave here, you will not be perfect either. While you shouldn't make mistakes because you can, mistakes will occur. When they do, repent according to 1 John 1:9 and ask the Lord to fill you fresh with his Holy Spirit. If it is a significant mistake, seek out your deliverance counselor, mentor, or discipleship leader for help.

Final Charge

Dear Friend—

More than anyone, God is proud of you for seeking him for a transformation in your life. God believes in you so very much; and not only God but also I believe in you and so does your counselor and those closest to you. You are clean! You are washed in the blood! You are ready for what is ahead! Glory to God and thanks be unto him for his wonderful mercy! The only thing left for you to do is to go forward in the mighty power of God's strength.

Now that you have moved on from your past, don't look back. Keep your eyes on what's ahead of you and focus your vision on Christ. Never forget what the Apostle Paul said:

> *No, dear brothers and sisters, I have not achieved it, but I focus on this one thing: Forgetting the past and looking forward to what lies ahead, I press on to reach the end of the race and receive the heavenly prize for which God, through Christ Jesus, is calling us. –Philippians 3:13-14*

Your new life awaits. You are going to do great…

Notes

Notes

Notes

Notes

Made in the USA
Lexington, KY
14 November 2016